Bullinger on ...

The Vail

The Leaven

The Church and Prayer

By E W Bullinger

ISBN: 978-1-78364-497-1

www.obt.org.uk

The Vail in the Temple

The Parable of the Leaven

The Church: Where to worship

Prayer: how to pray

The Open Bible Trust
Fordland Mount, Upper Basildon,
Reading, RG8 8LU, UK.

Bullinger on ...
The Vail, The Leaven, The Church and Prayer

Contents

THE
VAIL

THE VAIL

All Bible students are familiar with the beautiful vail which hung as a curtain dividing off effectually the Holy of Holies from the Holy Place, in the Tabernacle, and in the Temple; and separating the worshippers in the Holy Place from Him whom they worshipped, the glorious symbol of whose presence was in the Holy of Holies.[1]

That vail (we are told in Heb. 10:19, 20) represented the Flesh, or human body of the Lord Jesus.

It was a type of His humanity.

Do we all understand the Antitype? And discern the Lord's body; and know how, and in what way, the vail was its wonderful type?

We hear much, on every hand, of the new "Gospel of humanity," which teaches that everyone is a Christ and that Christ is humanity personified.

Sir Robert Anderson has powerfully shown[2] how much of the advancing Apostasy and the developing "Higher"

---

[1] See Ex. 26:31-34; 36:35, 36.
[2] Editor's note: see, for example, *Daniel in the Critic's Den* by Sir Robert Anderson.

Criticism is due to the gross ignorance of the Types of the Old Testament on the part of preachers and teachers. This is a solemn warning which ought to alarm all such; and stir us up to a more diligent and prayerful study of the Typical Teaching of the Word of God.

Of all the types, that of the beautiful vail of the Tabernacle and the Temple speaks most loudly in exposing and condemning the latest phase of the apostasy as shown in the Humanism of present day teaching.

Symbolically, the vail was intended to teach that Humanity, as such, could not approach God, who dwelt behind the vail.

This vail was a type of Christ's own perfect humanity; and it shut all other humanity out from God. The one side of it was illumined by artificial light and was seen by human eyes; the other side was illumined only by the glorious light, the *Schechina*, the symbol of God's presence.

It therefore was a fitting type of the blessed fact that Christ incarnate was perfect God and perfect man.

This two-fold perfection of Christ's manifestation on earth was an effectual witness to the impossibility of the access of humanity, as such, to God.

The object of a vail is *to hide*.

"Come not" was the warning which it continually gave forth (Lev. 16:2).

The perfect humanity of Christ is the only form of humanity which can approach without a vail to God; or which can dwell in the light of His glory; or can endure in that Divine light.

There can be no union therefore of man with Christ's humanity; no union in Incarnation.

The Incarnation of Christ, while it proclaims God, shuts out man.

Men might admire the beauty of that vail; as men may today admire the human character and the teaching of the earthly life of Christ. But the more perfect we find that humanity, the greater the evidence that it is totally distinct from man's.

The Incarnation, by itself (apart from the Redemption which was the purpose and object of it), neither brings man to God nor God to man.

True, it was "God with us," just as His Tabernacle was with men: but when the symbol of God's presence was with men, men could not have access to it. The beautiful vail was an effectual bar, and its one and only voice was "Come not."

The life of Christ on earth was an unceasing proclamation of the fact that only His humanity was shone upon by and dwelt in the glory of God.

"The Word was made flesh and dwelt among us (and we beheld His glory, as of the only begotten of the Father) full of grace and truth" (John 1:14).

The proclamation of His life ever was: - 'Except ye be holy, sinless, spotless, perfect, as I am, ye cannot enter into the presence of God.'

It was not the object of the vail to give access to God; for it was that which prevented it. Even so it was not the perfection of Christ's life on earth that brings us into the presence of God.

No! not until the blood of the sin offering had been sprinkled before the vail (Lev. 16:14, 19; 4:6, 7, 17), (blood which told that the sentence of death had been inflicted), could that vail be put aside, and entrance given to ordinary humanity into the presence of that glorious light.

It was not the beauty of the vail which made entrance possible, but the sprinkling of atoning blood before it.

That beauty might be admired by the worshipper; he might sing hymns in its praise; and give all sorts of sentimental and endearing names to it. He might use all kinds of poetical language in describing it; he might even copy it, and produce similar patterns of embroidery, or schemes of colour; but there was only one way of passing to the other side of it and of standing alive in the presence of God's glory; and that was *by sprinkling the blood before it and taking the blood of the victim beyond it.* This blood told of substitution and acknowledged that he who entered did so as a sinner, who had died and suffered the wages of his sin.

By no other means could he stand on the other side of that vail and live.

Its very stainlessness, though it might attract attention to it, repelled and kept the sinner from it.

The great antitypical lesson for us all is, that it is not by the beautiful life of Christ that we can enter into the presence of God.

It is not by any "imitation of Christ," not by the observance of any Rules for Daily Living, not by leading a religious or devout life, that we can pass beyond that vail.

To attempt it is to confess our ignorance of the very first letter of the Christian's alphabet; it is to own that we are destitute of the first fundamental lesson of the Christian life.

It is only when the precious blood of that perfect humanity of Christ had been shed that it avails us as our title to enter God's presence.

This is why, in 1 John 1:7, when speaking of our entrance into the light of God's presence and walking therein, that we are at once reminded of that blood, which alone gives us our title to enter, and preserves us alive, when we have entered into that presence.

"God is light . . . If we walk in the light, as He is in the light, we have fellowship one with another, and the blood of Jesus Christ His Son cleanseth us from all sin."

It is here and in this connection, that the cleansing power of the blood is mentioned; not in connection with sin or sinning. When it is a case of sin, then it is that we are reminded, not of the atoning blood of Christ, but of our Advocate with the Father. Then it is that we are simply assured of two facts: -

1. That relationship is not broken; God is still our Father: and

2. that Christ is our all-sufficient propitiation (1 John 2:1).

But it is in connection with approaching to and walking in the light of God's presence within the vail that we are reminded of the blood which must first be sprinkled before we can have either admission within or preservation when there (1 John 1:7).

Hence, it is not the life which Christ lived in His spotless humanity (still less our own imperfect copy of it) that gives us liberty to enter; but only when that humanity had been stained by His own blood atonement.

Then it is that we have

> "boldness to enter into the holiest, by the blood of Jesus, **by a newly slain and living way which He hath newly made** (or, opened) **for us, through the vail**, that is to say, His flesh" (Heb. 10:19, 20).

These words cannot be read too carefully or too thoughtfully. From them it is certain that our title to enter God's presence is not by the *earthly life* of Christ, but by the *sacrificial death* of Christ.

But the type in the Old Testament gives us only one part of the truth. It tells us only of *entrance* into the light, but not of abiding and "walking in the light." For this, the other part (the New Testament part) of the type was necessary.

When the perfect humanity of Christ had shed His atoning blood, then, at that very moment,

God rent that vail.

When the vail of Christ's human flesh was rent, then the vail of the Temple was rent.

God rent it Himself.

It was rent "from the top to the bottom."[3] Not from the bottom to the top. God rent it. He began where no man could reach it; and rent it with a power which no man could bring to bear upon it.[4]

Even so was Christ's flesh rent. Not by the hand of man: for, when the soldiers came to break His legs, they appeared surprised to find that He was "dead already" (John 19:33).

And thus, it was written:

---

[3] Matt. 27:50, 51. Mark 15:37 38.
[4] Jewish tradition tells us that the vail was so strong that two pairs of oxen attached to the opposite edges and driven in opposite directions, could not rend that vail.

"THOU hast brought me into the dust of death" (Ps. 22:15).

"All THY waves and THY billows are gone over me" (Ps. 42:7).

"It pleased the LORD to bruise Him" (Isa. 53:10).

"Awake, O sword, against MY shepherd" (Zech. 13:7).

The vail was rent at the moment that Christ died:

> "When He had cried again with a loud voice, He yielded up the ghost, and behold, the vail of the Temple was rent in twain from the top to the bottom" (Matt. 27:50, 51).

While the Lord Jesus lived, His perfect life was a barrier to our entrance into the light of God's presence.

It is precisely the same lesson as that which we have in John 12:23, 24: "Except a corn of wheat fall into, the ground AND DIE, it abideth alone: but if it die, it bringeth forth much fruit."

In His perfect and sinless humanity, He was, on the Divine side, ever abiding in the light of God's glory. But until He was "rent" it could be solemnly and truly said He "abideth alone."

If we are to have access into that glory, His flesh must be rent; and the rent vail furnishes the type.

It is when He dies, and when that perfect life is yielded up, that the way is open for our entrance, through our *union with Him in death and resurrection.*

Only then, and not until then, could there be "much fruit;" and thank God, we, by His grace, are part of that "much fruit" today.

The way into the holiest is now opened. "NOW, in Christ Jesus, ye who sometimes were far off are made nigh by the blood of Christ" (Eph. 2:13). Christ has already entered; and we are there in Him.

Ere long, we too shall follow; we even now enter by faith; and we shall soon enter, as He has done, in resurrection bodies, made like His own glorious body and be thus "received up in glory" to be "ever with the Lord." For this we wait.

> "Having, therefore, brethren, boldness to enter into the holiest by the blood of Jesus . . . let us draw near . . . in full assurance of faith" (Heb. 10:19-22).

LEAVEN

LEAVEN

"The Kingdom of Heaven is like unto leaven which a woman took, and hid in three measures of meal, till the whole was leavened." – Matt. 13:33.

In this short parable we have an example of a word[5] which, though it has a uniform rendering throughout the Bible, is yet, in one passage, generally taken in a sense which is exactly the opposite to all the others.

This is not a question of translation but of interpretation. It is not a question of grammar, but of consistency. It is in every passage translated "leaven"; but, while in some passages it is admittedly used in a bad sense, in others it is said to be doubtful; and in one passage, commentators, as a rule, agree in interpreting it in a good sense.

As this one passage is crucial to the interpretation of several parables, and has a most important practical bearing on the study of prophecy, it demands our careful consideration.

For, if leaven be understood here in a good sense, and the "church" substituted for the "kingdom," then we have to

---

[5] There are practically two words, the noun and the verb: (*zume*) *leaven;* and (*zumoo*) *to leaven.*

look forward to the triumph of Christianity, and to its universal extension until it Christianises the whole earth.

If, on the other hand, leaven be understood in a bad sense, then, whether the Church be substituted for the Kingdom or not, we have to look forward to universal corruption and general apostasy.

It will be seen at once that the correct understanding of this word is vital to a true interpretation not merely of this particular parable, but of the whole prophetic teaching of the Word of God. It is fundamental also to our whole practical Christian life.

For, if we hold the former to be true, we shall plunge into missionary work, and know nothing, but this as our absorbing object; while the least we can do is to give up our lives, and if need be, our life, in this great cause.

On the other hand, if we hold the latter to be true, we shall be witnesses to the Saviour whom God has provided for lost sinners (Acts 1:8); we shall "preach the Word; be instant in season and out of season" (2 Tim. 4:2); but, we shall do this understandingly. We shall not be lifted up with false hopes and vain expectations that men are going universally to receive it; but we shall preach the Word knowingly, being assured that "the time will come when men will not endure sound doctrine; but... shall turn their ears from the truth and be turned unto fables" (2 Tim. 4:3, 4).

So far from this being an incentive to idleness, it is revealed for the express purpose of inciting us to greater diligence; and is given as the very and only reason why we are to "preach the Word" with unceasing zeal.

It will be seen, therefore, that the true interpretation of the word "leaven" is fundamental and vital, not only to Christian doctrine, but to practical Christian service.

The truth will appear:

1. From the meaning of the word "leaven":
2. From its unvarying Biblical usage:
3. From the uniform testimony of Prophetic teaching.

1. From the meaning of the word "leaven"

As to the meaning of the word "leaven" there seems to be much confusion and inexactness. Probably, few Christians would be ready, off-hand, to answer the question, what is leaven? This suggestion can be tested by asking the first Christian whom one may meet. The answer, if correct, may be so, only "in part;" and in that case it will be incomplete.

Leaven, according to the dictionary, is "sour dough." But this will not do for us. We want to know why the dough should be sour? And how it became so.

To find this out, we have to avail ourselves of the latest scientific discoveries and definitions; using the word science in its true sense, as being *Scientia, i.e. what we know,* and not what we think.

It is a matter of common knowledge, even among the most ignorant races of mankind, that many liquors under certain conditions develop a process which we call fermentation, by which certain gases are given off and certain chemical changes take place.

To produce this, two things are necessary; viz., the presence of sugar, and exposure to the air. The latter is essential; for apart from this there can be no fermentation, whatever may be the sweetness of the liquor.

This tells us that the primal cause is in the air.

Observation has shown that there are two great classes of microscopic organisms in the air, which are known as "germs" and "ferments." We must not call the former animal, and the latter vegetable, though this would give a rough idea of the difference.
The differences, though microscopic, are definite; and sufficiently distinct for the various organisms to receive

names. These "ferments" are microscopic cells not more than 1/100 of a millimeter in diameter and are a species of fungi. They multiply with incredible rapidity by sporulation and budding; and not, as "germs" do, by fission and division. They are in the air, everywhere perhaps; but yet by no means equally distributed.

On coming in contact with a medium suitable for their propagation, they at once begin to multiply (and can thus be artificially cultivated under control). As the result of this action a scum rises to the surface of the liquor, which we call "yeast."[6] The germs of the yeast plant abound in the atmosphere of breweries, and in vineyards, especially at the vintage season.[7]

A little of this "yeast," on being put into dough, sets up fermentation in that; and changes it into a spongiform

---

[6] The English word "yeast" is the Ang. Sax. *gist*; Germ, *gascht* or *geist*. Hence our Eng. *gas*, and *gust* (of wind), and *ghost*. There may be a reference in this name to the working of some invisible power, like the "power of the air," exciting internal motion, and producing the effect of *foaming or frothing*.

Our English word *East* and *Easter* may be associated with *yeast*, from the *rising* caused by it.

[7] Milk also ferments, from a smaller kind of microscopic fungus than vineous ferments, called *Bacterium lactis*, which are cylindrical.

structure. This arises chiefly from the presence of carbonic acid gas.[8]

If some of this dough, while in this condition, be put into fresh dough, fermentation will be at once set up, and the "ferments" will be propagated in this way; just as plants can be propagated from cuttings or slips, as well as from the original seeds.

It is this fermented dough, put aside for future use, that is called "leaven."

A small piece of it is sufficient to reproduce the original fermentation throughout another mass of dough; so rapid is its growth and development.

In the case of grape-juice, the result, after the process of fermentation is completed, is what we know as wine. If fermentation has not taken place, it cannot rightly be called wine.[9]

---

[8] In the making of bread this gas is sometimes introduced artificially, by the use of *aerated* water or other devices, independently of yeast. It is then known as "Aerated bread."

[9] When it is bottled before fermentation is complete we get "sparkling" wine, on account of some of the carbonic acid gas remaining in it.

In the case of dough, it is different. Nothing but the heat of the oven can stop the process of fermentation. If it be not thus stopped, Bacteria would soon finish up the process and end it in putrefaction.[10]

2. From its unvarying Biblical usage

We are now in a position to understand the Biblical usage of the word "leaven."

In discovering this usage, all that is necessary for us to do is to look at every passage where it occurs; and see for ourselves, not what man says about it, but what God Himself teaches.
If there be any appropriateness in the symbols which God uses and have any connection between their nature and His lessons, then we have, already a sufficient indication of what is likely to be His usage of the symbol of leaven.

We must not, however, allow ourselves to be biased by this, though we must give it its due weight, and be ready to receive its evidence.

---

[10] Even so in the case of the corruption in the kingdom and in the Church: false doctrine starts the process, and then the putrefactive Bacteria represent all the degradation that follows as a natural sequence when the leaven has done all it can. Nothing but the fires of judgment will end it. For this it waits.

If we carefully note every reference to leaven in the Bible, we find: -

1. That it is used of its natural characteristics and effects as permeating the entire mass into which it is introduced: never ceasing in its action until the whole has been affected by its influence. This action is referred to in Matt. 13:33, Luke 13:21, 1 Cor. 5:6, Gal. 5:9 and Hosea 7:4.

2. Then it is used to describe the bread with which it is missed; and we have the terms "leavened bread" and "unleavened bread." This is referred to in Ex. 12:15, 19, 20, 34, 39; 13:3, 7.

3. Next, it is used in connection with Sacrifices; and, by the Divine ordinance, leaven was never to be offered with any offering made by fire unto the Lord.[11] This is referred to in Lev. 2:11; 6:17; 10:12.

---

[11] "Honey" also was forbidden *with the same limitation*, because it is a cause of fermentation. These two were only types; but their antitypes abound in the Hymn-books provided for our antitypical and spiritual "sacrifices of praise and thanksgiving." The *leaven* of false doctrine and the *honey* of human sentiment are everywhere to be found marring and defiling our Hymnology. But "God be not mocked," and these sacrifices are not accepted.

In the case of the Peace-offering (*not made by fire*), when offered as a "sacrifice of thanksgiving," it was to consist of "unleavened cakes:" but, beside the cakes, the offerer shall offer for HIS offering

4. Then we have the New Testament usage; which has reference to its moral application; from which it will be seen that the matters which are compared to the working of leaven are so likened because of its material characteristics.

(a) Doctrine. In Matt. 16:12 "the doctrine of the Pharisees and of the Sadducees" is likened to leaven.

In Mark 8:15 we are warned of "the leaven of the Pharisees, and of the leaven of Herod."

In Luke 12:1 we have "the leaven of the Pharisees, which is hypocrisy."

In Gal. 5:9 we have the doctrine of being "justified by the law" instead of by Christ, compared, in its working to the action of leaven.

All these doctrines are evil; and are condemned. There is no question about this; we have only to study these Scriptures to see why they are compared to leaven. We need not enlarge upon them, beyond noting that –

---

leavened bread with the sacrifice of thanksgiving of HIS peace offerings" (Lev. 7:12, 13).

This is a type of the evil which is inseparable from the sacrifices of praise and thanksgiving offered by human worshippers.

In the doctrine of the Sadducees we have Materialism, and in Pharisaism we have the doctrines of Plato, which are preserved in Traditional Psychology, and are the seeds of Spiritism.

In combination with the leaven of the Pharisees, which is hypocrisy – (*i.e.,* the form without the power) – we have "the leaven of Herod," which is the same in its outward aspect. Herod could be religious, and he "heard John gladly," and "did many things" (Mark 6:20); and yet, a little later, he could only do one thing, for "he sent and beheaded John in the prison" (*v.* 27). Even so today, we have those who have only the "form of godliness without the power." They can flock to *hear* a preacher and *do* many things; they have been leavened with "the leaven (or doctrine) of the Pharisees, and with the leaven of Herod." (Compare Mark 4:16, 17.)

(b) Practice. Our association with evil-doers is compared to the fatal working of leaven: inasmuch as the danger of the whole lump's being leavened by the presence of such is great. (Compare 1 Cor. 15:33.) The "old leaven" is to be purged out. The whole of the context (1 Cor. 5.) should be read, to understand the special instruction of verses 6-8.

5. Finally, we have the usage in three remaining passages in which the *bad* sense of the word is questioned, and a good sense is suggested, viz.: -

(a) Lev. 23:17.

(b) Amos 4:4, 5.

(c) Matt. 13:33.

(a) Lev. 23:15-17 "Ye shall count unto you from the morrow after the sabbath from the day that ye brought the sheaf of the wave offering; seven sabbaths shall be complete: . . . Ye shall bring out of your habitations two wave loaves of two tenth deals: they shall be of fine flour; *they shall be baken with leaven*; they are the firstfruits unto the Lord."

This is all explained to us in 1 Cor. 15:23: "Christ the firstfruits." This is "the wave sheaf" of Lev. 23:10-14.[12]

"Afterward, they that are Christ's at His coming." These arc the "two wave loaves" of Lev. 23:15-21.[13]

"Then cometh the end." This is the harvest" of *v.* 22.

We have the antitypes of these Gospels and Acts. The first type, the wave sheaf, had been accomplished in the Resurrection of Christ.

_____

[12] The Septuagint has (*harpage*), *first-fruit (v.* 10).

[13] The Septuagint has (*protogennema*), *first-begotten* (v. 17). This is a truly beautiful commentary: almost like an inspiration.

Fifty days after the Resurrection began the fulfilment of the second type – in the proclamation to "Repent" (Acts 2:38; 3:19-26, R.V.); and in the then readiness of Christ to come. Had that command to repent been obeyed, the promise made to them and to their children must have been fulfilled. Christ's promised coming would have been fulfilled in the sending of Jesus Christ. In this case, "the first resurrection" must then have taken place.

But we know that Israel did not repent. The two houses of the "men of Judah" and the "men of Israel" had both been called by Peter: first separately (Acts 2:14, 22) and then together (v. 36, "all the house of Israel").[14] But they refused that call. Hence the Kingdom and the coming King, and the foretold "first resurrection" are all, now in abeyance.

"All things are to be put under His feet" (1 Cor. 15:25). But now, "we see not yet all things put under Him" (Heb. 2:8).

The type however, is still true, and will one day be verified in its antitype.

---

[14] Editor's note: Some modern commentators talk about the lost tribes of Israel but Peter here, and especially Paul (Acts 26:7) see all Twelve Tribes as one.

Now we can understand *why there was to be leaven in those "two wave loaves."* For, though they were made of the very flour of the first fruits: though Christ partook of the same nature, and was of the same seed of Abraham, yet He was "without sin" (Heb. 4:15); He "knew no sin" (2 Cor. 5:21); He "did no sin" (1 Peter 2:22; "and in Him is no sin" (1 John 3:5): yet, because the "two wave loaves" were the type of His earthly people who were all "under sin" (Rom. 3:9), and who cannot say "we have no sin" (1 John 1:8), *leaven* is expressly ordered to be mixed, in order to make the type correspond with the antitype.

Not only is this the case, but with both the "wave sheaf" and the "two wave loaves" certain offerings were to be made.

But while, in the case of the "wave sheaf." we have only two: "the burnt offering," and "the meal offering with the drink offering thereof" (Lev. 23:12-14), yet in the case of the "two wave loaves" we have four offerings: - the burnt offerings, "the meal offering and their drink offerings," *"the sin offering,"* and the peace offering" (*vs.* 18-20).

Thus, beside the presence of sin in the people being typified by the presence of "leaven" in the "two wave loaves," that sin was further shown to be there by *the sin offering* which is associated with *them*, though not with "the wave sheaf."

This is conclusive as to Lev. 23:17.

(b) With regard to Amos 4:4, 5. This is either the language of irony; or it refers to the special form of peace offering, offered as a "thanksgiving with leaven," prescribed in Lev. 7:14, as a type of the sin even in the thanksgiving of the offerer. (See note, above.)

(c) There remains only Matt. 13:33. Can it be believed that, in this one passage, the word "leaven" is used in the very opposite sense to that in which we find it in all the other passages?

And yet every commentator of repute, without any hesitation, would not only authorise us so to interpret it, but does not hesitate to bid us so to understand it.

But we cannot do so; no one has such authority, neither have we any such liberty.

The parable is usually read according to its punctuation, which is, of course entirely human and incorrect. The parable does not say

"THE KINGDOM OF HEAVEN IS LIKE UNTO LEAVEN."

But ...

"THE KINGDOM OF HEAVEN IS LIKE
unto leaven which a woman took,
and hid in three measures of meal,
till the whole was leavened."

It is not merely the substance of "leaven," or the initial act of the woman, but it is *the whole process* even up to the final leavening of the whole to which the Kingdom of Heaven was likened.

In this the parable has its place, both in logical relationship and in its doctrinal teaching, with the other parables with which it stands in immediate connection.

It is the last of the first four spoken to the multitude "out of the house" (*v.* 1), which have a common lesson, quite distinct from that *of the last three, which were spoken to the disciples "in the house" v.* 34).[15]

In the *first* (the Sower), only one portion of the seed brought forth fruit; and there is no limitation as to the seed sown on the other three portions bringing forth any fruit.

In the *second* (the Tares), the "enemy" secretly sowed by night the seed of the tares. These are "the children of the wicked one," and they continue in the field, which is the

---

[15] See *The Kingdom and the Church*, by the Editor. Originally published by Eyre and Spottiswoode, 33 Paternoster Row.

world (*cosmos*), and defiling it, until the time of the harvest, which is the end of the age (*aion*).

In the *third* (the Mustard Tree), we see "the fowls of the air" (the same evil creatures as in the first parable), finding a home in its branches.

In the *fourth* (the Leaven), we see the same corrupting influence at work, invisibly, like "ferments"; in contrast with what is visible, as in the proceeding parable of the Tree.

Can we doubt that we have one and the same lesson in each of these four parables?

"The wicked one" in the first, limits the reception of the good seed.

The same power, the "enemy," mixes his own seed with the children of the Kingdom.

The same power (for the fowls mean the wicked one, compare *v.* 4 with *v.* 19), takes up his abode in the Kingdom (compare Rev. 18:2).

It is therefore the same power that we see in the woman and her work.

The seed is sown not in the world, but only in four kinds of "ground" in it.

The seed, though sown in the world, has tares mixed with the whole of it.

The mustard tree is not the world, for it is only rooted in it.

So likewise, it is not the world which is permeated by the leaven, but only the "meal" which is in it.

The Lord afterward repeated two of these parables (the Mustard Tree and the Leaven) in Luke 13:18-21. The occasion which called forth the repetition, marked by the word "then" (v. 18), shows that they were used to illustrate the increasing hostility of His enemies, which was the working of the leaven.

If the Lord, in His teaching, meant us to understand that the *whole world* was to be permeated with that which is good, He would have pictured to us (in the first) the seed everywhere producing fruit and the ground all "good." He would have spoken (in the second) of an unmixed field, sown only with good seed; or of the tares being changed into wheat. He would have shown (in the third) a tree affording no shelter for unclean and hateful birds; and (in the fourth) some type other than leaven, seeing that the

Holy Spirit in the Word, and He Himself in all His subsequent teaching, used it only of that which is evil.

Those who interpret the leaven as being typical of the Gospel do violence to the whole of these four parables as well as to the whole analogy of Bible truth. For the Word is in no sense hidden but is to be everywhere preached. The Gospel is to be everywhere proclaimed with all boldness. If the Gospel be *hidden*, it is the work of "the god of this world" (2 Cor. 4:3, 4).

3. From the uniform testimony of Prophetic teaching.

Only a few words are necessary to show how all this agrees with the unvarying testimony of Prophetic teaching.

Everywhere are we warned of judgment to come; of dark days and "perilous times" (2 Tim. 3:1); of "evil men, and deceivers waxing worse and worse" (2 Tim. 3:13); of "departure from the Faith" (1 Tim. 4:1); of "scoffers walking after their own lusts" (2 Pet. 3:3); of the coming "apostasy" and the revelation of "the man of sin" (2 Thess. 2:3). Everywhere are we warned against the spread of doctrinal corruption and of fleshly lusts.

Instead of being told that the world is not good enough for the coming of Christ, we are told that it is not bad enough. Instead of being told that He will not appear until the world's conversion comes, we are told that it will not be until the apostasy shall have come (2 Thess. 2:3).

Instead of the Church overcoming the world, we see before our very eyes that the world is fast overcoming the Church.

Truly the leaven is working in the Church as well, as it has worked, and will ere long again work, in the Kingdom. For the prophecies and the parables of the Kingdom leap over this present Church interval and continue its history as though the Church had no existence. And the work of this leaven is only evil.

Our attitude, therefore, now, toward God and His sure word of prophecy; toward man, the Church, and the world; is entirely dominated by the sense in which we understand the Bible use of the word "leaven." This will be a sufficient reason for our having devoted so much space to the consideration of the subject.

More on Parables

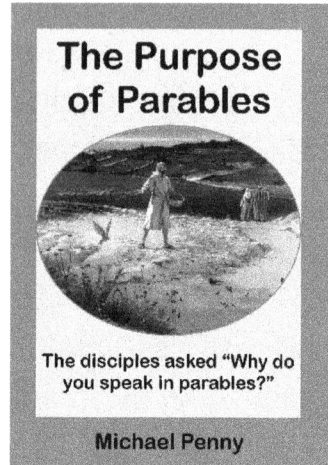

Pondering Parables
The TEN VIRGINS
GREAT BANQUET
Charles Ozanne

The Purpose of Parables

The disciples asked "Why do you speak in parables?"

Michael Penny

Pondering Parables by Charles Ozanne

The Purpose of Parable by Michael Penny

Further details of these books can be seen on **www.obt.org.uk** and they are available from that website and from:

The Open Bible Trust,
Fordland Mount, Upper Basildon,
Reading, RG8 8LU, UK.

They are also available as eBooks from Amazon and Apple and as KDP paperbacks from Amazon.

THE CHURCH: WHERE TO WORSHIP

THE CHURCH: WHERE TO WORSHIP

Several inquirers have asked us, from time to time, as to where and with whom they ought to worship.

We have hitherto refrained from answering such questions, because we are not directors of the conscience, but ministers of the Word. However, we have lately read *Two Letters*, written by Mr. A. N. Groves in 1834 and 1836, which have been so helpful to ourselves, that we feel we ought to pass them on to others. They are too long for reproduction here, so that we shall have to be content with a few extracts, and must condense the rest in our own words, omitting what is purely ephemeral and personal. We ought, however, to state, to make the words more intelligible, that Mr. Groves was associated with Mr. J. G. Bellett and T. N. Darby in 1827, in Dublin and Plymouth; and that one of the letters is addressed to the latter; while Mr. Bellett and others always spoke of Mr. Groves as "the father of these principles," which united them in fellowship.

The subject is entitled: *Catholic Christianity and Party Communion,* and they deal with *"the principles of union and communion in the Church of God."*

"Let us then for a moment dwell on the principles that ought to regulate our intercourse as Christians, of whatever sect or name, and examine to what extent we are *free*, and to what extent *bound;* or rather what are the limits within which our communion with an individual as a Christian, or a body of individuals in public worship is to be confined." The principles of communion of the church on earth must be those which shall prevail in Heaven; and the more nearly they assimilate now, the more perfect they will be.

What are those principles? *Loving all whom Christ loves, because they bear His impress.* If it be asked how are these to be distinguished? We may look for the Holy Ghost to help us. If it be asked what is to be done with their errors? These are no bar to communion, unless they bar Christ from the erring brother's heart. While we hope Christ lingers, let us linger; and rather be behind than before, to quit; in pitiful remembrance of our own iniquities and unnumbered errors. So long as we judge Christ to be dwelling with a man, that is our warrant for receiving him; and for the charity of that judgment that declares Him not there, we are responsible. But we must stay on the ground given by Peter, seeing God has given him the like gift He has given unto us. Who are we that we should withstand God? And as to his errors, we must bear them, and, seeing they cannot be removed from *us*. (till, with sorrow, they are removed from *him*) we must bear this burden for the Lord's sake, for our brother's sake, and for our own sake; remembering that, perhaps while we are bearing his burdens, he is bearing ours and thus we are mutually fulfilling the law of Christ in bearing them for each other. We are to love and bear with him, because Christ does, be other things as they may.

Then, as to communion with congregations, we must consider ourselves in the double position (1) of individuals who have duties to ourselves and (2) of members of the Body of Christ, an immense brotherhood, embracing the universal church throughout the world, in all the congregations of the saints, where Christ still walks amidst the golden candlesticks, notwithstanding unnumbered weaknesses and errors.

Our first duty in selecting the congregation with whom we should worship should be to consider where the form is most Scriptural; where the ministrations are most spiritual; where there is the sweetest savour of Christ; where our own souls are most instructed in the Word: and where the Holy Spirit is most manifestly present with those who minister and those who hear.

As to our liberty in Christ, to worship with any congregation under heaven where God manifests Himself to save and to bless, can there be in any Christian mind, a doubt? If my Lord should say to me in any of the many congregations of the church: "What doest Thou here?" I would reply: "Seeing Thou wert here to save and sanctify, I felt it would be safe to be with Thee." If He again said (as indeed He may among most of us): "Dids't Thou not see abominations here, an admixture of that which was un-Scriptural and the absence of that which was Scriptural, and in some points error, at least in your judgment?" My answer would be: "Yea, Lord; but I dared not call that place unholy, where Thou wert present to bless; nor by refusing communion in worship, reject those as unholy whom Thou hadst by Thy saving power evidently sanctified and set apart for Thine own."

Our reason for rejecting corporate bodies is that God doth not manifest Himself among them, though He may pluck some individuals as brands from the burning. To these we cry, standing on the outside: "Come out of her, my people; come out of her."

Among the others, we stand with Christ *in the midst*. We would linger, with the Lord, in testimony rather than cry like Edom in the days of Judah's sorrow – "Down with her, down with her, even to the ground."

To the question, are we not countenancing error by this plan? Our answer is, that, if we must appear to countenance error, or to discountenance brotherly love, we prefer the former, hoping that our lives and our tongues may be allowed by the Lord, so intelligibly to speak, that at last our righteousness shall be allowed to appear. But, if not, we may feel we have chosen the better part, since we tarried only for our Lord's departure.

But so long as Christ dwells in an individual, or the Holy Spirit works in the midst of a congregation, blessing the ministrations to the conversion and edification of souls, we dare not denounce, or formally withdraw from either, for fear of the awful sin of schism, of sin against Christ and His Mystical Body.

If we depart from these fundamental principles, we shall, instead of standing forth as witnesses *for the truth*, be standing forth as witnesses *against error* and have lowered ourselves from heaven to earth in our position as witnesses.

Let our aim be to manifest forth that *life* we have received from Christ by seeking to find that life in others; so that, as Christ has received them, should we also to the glory of God the Father. Let us share with them in *part*, though we cannot in *all*, their services. In fact, as we have received them for their *life*, we cannot reject them for their systems.

The moment the witnessing for the common life as our *bond* gives place to a witnessing *against* errors, by separation of persons, that moment the narrowest and most bigoted mind amongst us will rule, and the enlarged heart will yield before the narrowest conscience; while light, and not *life*, will be the measure of communion.

It is surely better to bear with their evils, than to separate from their good.

It is useless to force others to *act* in uniformity further than they *feel* uniformity. Otherwise we merely afford a ready outlet to the propensities of the flesh under the appearance of spiritual authority and zeal for the truth.

And the end of it all will be that, though only brethren in a Father's house, many will exercise more than a Father's power, without a Father's heart of mercy.

Some of Mr. Groves' words are almost prophetic. He says that where all this is the case; where others have *grown up* in this system, without being *led into it* through suffering and sorrow, there will be felt, overwhelmingly, the authority of men; who will be known more by what they *witness against* than what they *witness for*; and that, practically, this will, in the end, prove that they witness against all except themselves, having a Shibboleth, which, though it may be *different* from all others, will be just as *real*.

More on the church

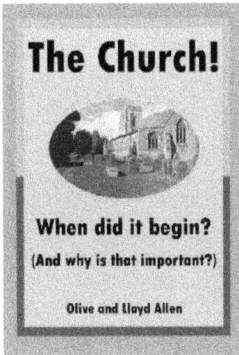

The Church! When did it begin?
(And why is that important?)

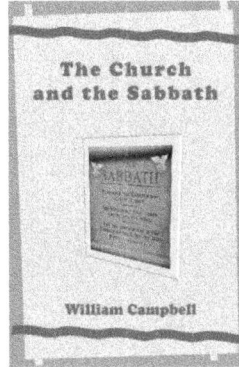

The Church and the Sabbath

William Campbell

The Church! When did it begin?
(And why is that important?)
By Olive and Lloyd Allen

The Church and the Sabbath
By William Campbell

****

Further details of these books can be seen on **www.obt.org.uk** and they are available from that website and from:

The Open Bible Trust,
Fordland Mount, Upper Basildon,
Reading, RG8 8LU, UK.

They are also available as eBooks from Amazon and Apple and as KDP paperbacks from Amazon.

PRAYER

PRAYER

Prayer is the breath of the New Nature; as the Word of God is its food.

In the natural world of physiology, we do not concern ourselves with the phenomena of digestion, but with obtaining and partaking of our food. It is a sign of an abnormal condition of things, if we occupy ourselves with the analysis of our food, or with the process of digestion.

So, with our breathing. Our one concern, physiologically, is to obtain pure air, and to breathe it. If we trouble ourselves with the act of breathing itself, we should soon be afraid to breathe at all.

So long as we think nothing about either, we both eat and breathe, while we unconsciously carry out the laws of physiology.

It is even so in the spiritual world. If we content ourselves with analyzing and describing the Word of God we shall never "grow thereby." If we would be properly nourished by it, we must actually feed upon it each one for himself. It will not strengthen us merely to listen to addresses about food, or on the art of carving it – we must partake of it ourselves and "inwardly digest it."

So with prayer. It is the breath of the New Nature[16]. The moment we think about how we ought to breathe, or occupy ourselves with what breathing is, instead of breathing, we must sink and die.

In like manner, when we substitute the consideration of what prayer is, or ought to be; or when, or how it should be made; or have to search for suitable words to express the prayer, it ceases to serve its purpose, and is no longer the cause of effect of true spiritual vitality.

- Breathing is at once the effect and the cause of natural life.
- Prayer is at once the cause and maintenance of spiritual life.

To be real, it must be the outcome of the possession of spiritual life. It must be spiritually spontaneous, and as much without artificial plan and design, as our natural breathing is.

---

[16] For more on this see *The Two Natures in the Child of God* by E W Bullinger, published by The Open Bible Trust: details towards the end of this book.

The moment it is otherwise, it ceases to be real prayer. Prayer, therefore, does not necessarily require *words*.

- It may be only the *breathing* of the New Nature (Lam. 3:55, 56), but it is heard.
- It may be only the *groaning*, as of Israel in Ex. 2:23, a., but it is heard.
- It may be only a *cry*, as of David in Ps. 57:3, but it is heard.
- It may be only the inward *unuttered cry*, as of Moses in Ex. 14:15. But it is heard and understood.
- It may be only the *thought* of those who hear the LORD (Mal. 3:16). But "the LORD hearkened and heard."

In other words, prayer is occupation of the spirit with God. It is having to do with Him.

Hence, it is that we so often find it expressed by the word "cry."

In the New Testament, in all but two places,[17] it is one of two words; the former has regard to the *power* of Him with whom we have to do; while the latter marks our own *need* and *insufficiency* and has regard to our special *necessity*.

---

[17] 1 Tim. 4:5, and Jas. 5:15.

This is why we are told to pray. It is not that God needs anything from us. It is not that He is ignorant of our needs, and thoughts, and desires. But prayer is meant to force us into the place of helplessness. It is meant to put us before the mighty God with our faces in the dust, confessing in ourselves we are nothing and have nothing and can do nothing; but that our only hope and help is in God: that, in ourselves we can show no merit, no reason, no cause why we should have the least of His mercies, but that all must come from God to us through pure, free, sovereign grace. Not on account of the worthiness of our prayers (for that would at once be a ground of merit), but only because He is "the God of all grace."

This is beautifully illustrated by David in Psalm 57. The character of

The Person Praying

is shown by the opening words.

> "Be merciful unto me, O God,
> Be merciful unto me."

The repetition emphasises the depth of his need, and of his destitution of spiritual things.

Those who know the place in which the very act of prayer is meant to put them, cannot boast of any stock of grace, for God does not entrust them with the keeping of it.

They come, and this is the burden of their cry:

"Nothing in my hand I bring."

They say (Ps. 57:3):

"I will cry unto God most high."

It is not begging, as though one knew what to ask, that we have here. Babes cry! And no plea is so strong with a mother. It is more so with Him who hearkens to the cry of His people; the groan of the oppressed in the pit of corruption; the moan of those who are robbed and spoiled and have "fallen among thieves." These call forth the concern, the care and help of "the good Samaritan," the "brother born for adversity," the High Priest who "has compassion on the ignorant and on them who are out of the way."

Some may object to being brought down so low, but those who know anything of "God most high," will thankfully take their place of man, most low.

Some may say this is bringing man down to the level of the beasts! But no: Fallen man is below that level already.

Beasts can be tamed by man; they can be made useful and obedient; but, fallen man by nature is "enmity against God. He is not subject to the law of God, neither indeed can be" (Rom. 8:7): *i.e.*, not of himself, but grace can search him and deal with him. Of Israel Jehovah said:

> "The ox knoweth his owner,
> And the ass his master's crib;
> But Israel doth not know,
> My people doth not consider." (Isa 1:3).

Others may object and say we are making man a mere machine! We do nothing so great and good as that.

Man is nothing half as good as a machine. Look at a beautiful and complicated piece of machinery. See how marvelously and perfectly and exquisitely it carries out unerringly the will of him who made it. See how it performs exactly what its maker designed and planned. Where is man compared with this? Where were our first parents? Where is man, with all his education and religion? Does man always carry out the will of his Creator? Does man ever carry out the designs and plans of his Maker? No! Man is a mass of ruin and not a machine. He is like a broken machine that is only a heap of broken, tangled rods and bands and wheels, utterly unable to perform his Maker's will.

Saved sinners, who have come under the power of the wondrous invincible grace of God, have discovered their own unworthiness and the glory of the grace of God. They have realised their own helplessness. They know something of the assaults of Satan, the hatred of the world and the enmity of the flesh and they say with David,

"I will cry unto God most High."

They have had it revealed to them, that He who is now God most High, for their sakes became man most low: came like the good Samaritan "where he (the lost one) was"; attends to all his concerns; and provides and secures all needful blessings for him.

God most High is the God who "performeth [*all things*] for me," David says. Notice that "*all things*" is in italics. The ellipsis is left for each one to fill in the blank according to his need. It is like Ps. 138:8.

"The Lord will perfect [*that which*] concerneth me."

Various translators have filled in the words according to their own ideas, one supplies the word "purposes"; another, "His mercy"; others, "His promises," or, "my desires." Luther supplies "my sorrow."

But it is needless for us to supply anything. If we supply one thing we necessarily shut out other things. A good word to supply would be the Saviour's own word "Whatsoever[18] (John 14:13) . . . . I will do it."

And note, it does not say I will enable you to do it. No! it is better than that: it is "I will do it." It is "God who performeth [all things] for me."

Many believers want to perform their own things for themselves and ask only for a little enabling help.

Others only want God to perform certain definite things for them. They thus "limit God."

Oh! how many there are today who fall into His People's sin when they "limited the Holy one of Israel." (Ps. 78:41).

What a snare is this! We see only one way of help or blessing, or deliverance: and we ask for that. We know not how many better ways the Lord has in His infinite wisdom. We know of one way, and we "limit" Him by asking for this, to our own hindrance and hurt.

---

[18] For more on this verse and the meaning of *whatsoever* see chapters 19 and 20 of *40 Problem Passages* by Michael Penny, published by The Open Bible Trust.

Oh, let us beware of limiting the Holy one of Israel!

Prayer is meant to humble us, and to put us into the low place before "God most high," and we – yes – the old nature in the best of us, turn that low place into a throne from which we dictate to God what He shall do for us or for others: what He shall do at home or in Africa, or India or China.

We, who cannot manage our own affairs – (for not one of us has managed them as he *wishes* he had), we do not hesitate to take on us the affairs of the universe and ask for this and that to be done here and there. We could not do less, if we were omniscient!

If any ask us whether we are not "definite in our prayer"? We reply – We would be if we were omniscient! We would be if we did not fear to limit the Infinite, Almighty, God.

Oh! how blessed to have to do with "God most high," "God that performeth all things for me." God, who knoweth what is best.

If we knew anything of His infinite wisdom, of His infinite power, of His infinite love, we should not be occupying ourselves with our own "surrender"; but we should be crying to "God most high," to perform His will for us, and to do whatsoever He pleases. And, this is not some point which we hope ultimately to reach; but it is the point which we should start from, the low place. No one can imagine what the blessed end of peace and rest would be, which is reached from such a starting place. No one can realise the fulness of meaning involved in the possession of "God that performeth all things for me"; or of the Saviour's words "I will do it."

The lowest place is the place where we shall hear His voice saying:

> "I HAVE CAUSED thine iniquity to pass from thee,
> And I WILL CLOTHE thee with change of raiment" (Zech. 3:4).

When thus cleansed and clothed we shall sing, "HE HATH CLOTHED me with the garments of Salvation". (Isa. 61:10).

When fainting by the way, we shall hear His word;

> "HE MAKETH me to lie down . . .
> "HE PREPARETH a table for me . . . (Ps. 23:2, 5).

When our heart is hard, we shall remember that "GOD MAKETH my heart soft and the Almighty troubleth me" (Job 23:16).

When we feel our unprofitableness, we shall remember and say, "Lord, THOU HAS WROUGHT all our works in us" (Isa. 26:12).

When, like Mephibosheth, we are in the land of "no pasture" (LoDebar) and yearning for the presence and favour of the King, we shall remember the word, that is written:

"Then King David SENT and FETCHED him."

Ah! "God most High" is our God; the God who performeth all things for us. "The God of all grace."

Grace that sends for and fetches us.
Grace that cleanses and clothes us.
Grace that brings and carries us.
Grace that feeds and satisfies us.

Truly we may say with David, "I will cry unto God most high, unto God that performeth all things for me."

More on Prayer

Some of the sentiments expressed in this chapter are not found in later writings by E W Bullinger. He was not afraid to change some of his teaching as he developed his understanding of the Scriptures, and especially when he realised that Israel did not lose its prime position in God's working with mankind until then end of Acts when God's salvation was sent to the Gentiles independently of the Jews (Acts 28:25-28). It was then that the Church, which is the Body of Christ, commenced, a subject found in the letters written after that time: namely Ephesians, Philippians, Colossians, 1 & 2 Timothy, Titus, Philemon. And Bullinger did write another book on prayer based on one of these later letters.

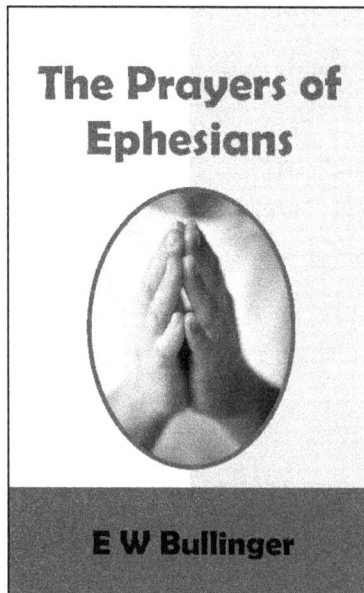

The Prayers of Ephesians

E W Bullinger

The Prayers of Ephesians
By E W Bullinger

There are two longer prayers recorded in the Epistle to the Ephesians, plus a short concluding prayer. They are not merely human compositions, but rather "the Divine breathings and groanings of the Holy Spirit" says the author. As such they are inexhaustible in their fulness and depth.

Many of us struggle with prayer. This is because we know neither the height of the Father's power and love, nor the depth of our own need. So here we are prayed for.

The two longer prayers are recorded in Ephesians 1:15-23, and 3:14-21. While these two prayers are in every way different and distinct, and are full of contrast, yet there is one subject that is common to both: namely Christ Jesus, our Saviour, Head and Lord.

In the former prayer the subject is Christ, and what God has made Him to be unto His people. In the latter prayer it is Christ, and what God has made us to be in Him. In the former it is - **we in Christ**. In the latter it is - **Christ in us**. In the former it is God's power which He wrought *in Christ:* in the latter it is the Father's power that works *in us*.

All Christians, of whatever persuasion, will be greatly blessed by reading this publication and by meditating upon *The Prayers of Ephesians.* This is Bullinger at his best. A wonderful exposition.

Further details of this book, and the ones one the next pages, can be seen on www.obt.org.uk and they are available from that website and from:

The Open Bible Trust,
Fordland Mount, Upper Basildon,
Reading, RG8 8LU, UK.

They are also available as eBooks
from Amazon and Apple
and as KDP paperbacks
from Amazon.

Also on Prayer

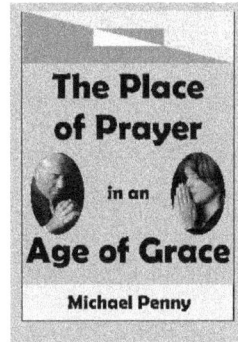

Prayer that is Powerful and Effective
By Andrew Morton

The different words used in the Word of God and rendered "pray", "prayer", "make supplication" and "make intercession", etc., indicate to us something of the many-sidedness of prayer.

In order to gain a comprehensive view of what God means by "prayer" (and prayer that is "powerful and effective"), the author considers the seventeen different Hebrew words used in the Old Testament for prayer.

And he also helpfully considers the prayer-life of many of God's children, which is detailed in Scripture for our learning. This has been recorded not merely for our interest, but rather our edification and for the deepening of our own prayer life.

Unanswered Prayer
by Neville Stephens,

One of the most perplexing problems facing Christians today is why they do not see more answers to their prayers or, to be more accurate, why they do not see more positive answers to their intercessions.

In this publication Neville Stephens considers the prayers of the New Testament and comes to the conclusion that those of Peter, John, James and Jude and those contained in the Gospels are very different from those of the Apostle Paul. His solution to Unanswered Prayer will be of interest to every thinking Christian.

The Place of Prayer in an Age of Grace
by Michael Penny

Within Christendom there is a wide variety of teaching on prayer. Anyone who has studied this subject from the pages of the New Testament will not be surprised by this. As we progress through the Scripture we find different teaching on prayer, and we find different promises associated with prayer. Indeed, at times we find no promises associated with prayer!

In the Gospels, and in the letters written to the Jewish Christians of the Acts period (Hebrews, James, 1 & 2 Peter, 1, 2 & 3 John, Jude and Revelation), we find a definiteness associated with prayer. We find promises and we find the world "will" associated with prayer. If we base our prayer expectation upon such passages as these, not only may we be disappointed, we can become judgmental - of ourselves and of others. We begin to think that our prayers are not answered because we don't seek His kingdom first (Matthew 6:33), or because the people praying are not right with God (James 5:26). We may be wiser basing our prayer expectations of those apart of Scripture written for Gentiles living in this age of grace.

That is what this book seeks to do, and it does so by a series of question and answers based upon the last seven letters of Paul; Ephesians, Colossians, Philemon, Philippians, Titus 1 & 2 Timothy. These were the letters Paul wrote after Acts 28:25-28, after the nation of Israel had lost its central position in God's plan, and after God had turned to the Gentiles, independently of Israel. In these letters we have essential teaching on prayer for this age of grace in which we live.

ABOUT THE AUTHOR

Ethelbert W. Bullinger D.D. (1837-1913) was a direct descendant of Heinrich Bullinger, the great Swiss reformer who carried on Zwingli's work after the latter had been killed in war.

E. W. Bullinger was brought up a Methodist but sang in the choir of Canterbury Cathedral in Kent. He trained for and became an Anglican (Episcopalian) minister before becoming Secretary of the Trinitarian Bible Society. He was a man of intense spirituality and made a number of outstanding contributions to biblical scholarship and broad-based evangelical Christianity.

The following is a selection of works by E W Bullinger published by The Open Bible Trust

The Transfiguration
The Knowledge of God
God's Purpose in Israel

The Prayers of Ephesians
The Lord's Day (Revelation 1:10)
The Rich Man and Lazarus
The Importance of Accuracy
Christ's Prophetic Teaching
The Resurrection of the Body
The Divine Names and Titles
The Spirits in Prison: 1 Peter 3:17-4:6
The Lesson of the Book of Job: The Oldest Lesson in the World
The Seven Sayings to the Woman at the Well
The Foundations of Dispensational Truth
The Christian's Greatest Need
Introducing the Church Epistles
The Two Natures in the Child of God
The Name of Jehovah in the Book of Esther
The Names and Order of the Books of the Old Testament
The Second Advent in Relation to the Jew
The Vision of Isaiah: Its Structure and Scope
The Importance of Accuracy: in the study of the Bible
The Man of God
The Road to Holiness
Sanctification and Perfection
Bullinger on ... The Vail, The Leaven, The Church and Prayer

All the above are available as eBooks from Amazon and Apple and as KDP paperbacks from Amazon.

BULLINGER'S LAST BOOK

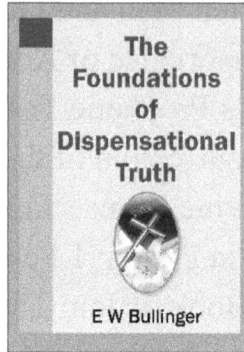

The Foundations of Dispensation Truth

Bullinger's last book, reflecting his mature views.

This is Bullinger's last book and is his definitive work on the subject of dispensationalism. It covers the ministries of ...

- the prophets,
- the Son of God,
- those that heard Christ, and
- the ministry of Paul, the Apostle to the Gentiles.

He comments on the Gospels and the Pauline epistles and has a lengthy section on the Acts of the Apostles, followed by one explaining why miraculous signs of the Acts period ceased.

This is a newly typeset book, well presented in an easy to read format.

Copies of
The Foundations of Dispensational Truth,
and ALL of the books listed on the next
pages, are available from

www.obt.org.uk

and from

The Open Bible Trust,
Fordland Mount, Upper Basildon,
Reading, RG8 8LU.

They also available as eBooks
from Amazon Kindle and Apple,
and as KDP paperbacks from Amazon.

The Vail, The Leaven, The Church and Prayer 72

ALSO BY BULLINGER

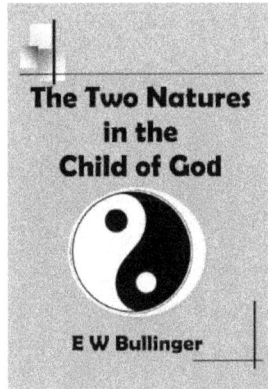

The Two Natures in the Child of God

The Bible sees the Christian as having an 'old nature', inherited through generation from Adam, and a 'new nature', bestowed through regeneration by God.

The names and characteristics of each are many and various, including "the natural man" and "the old man" over against "the divine nature" and "the new man".

The conflict between the two natures is discussed with details of our responsibilities regarding each, and the ultimate end of the old and new natures. Finally, practical suggestions are made for dealing with the old nature.

Available as an eBook from Amazon and Apple and as a KDP paperback from Amazon.

ABOUT THIS BOOK

Bullinger on ...

The Vail, The Leaven, The Church and Prayer

E W Bullinger was a dedicated student of the Word and a prolific writer. As well as writing several major books and compiling *The Companion Bible*, he wrote dozens of shorter articles and pamphlets. In this publication we have put together four interesting and helpful the topics.

- The Vail in the Temple, which was torn from top to bottom.
- The Parable of the Leaven.
- Churches! Where should we worship?
- Prayer. How do we prayer and what should be pray for?

We trust that the reader will, as with all Bullinger's writing, find much food for study and contemplation.

Publications of The Open Bible Trust must be in accordance with its evangelical, fundamental and dispensational basis. However, beyond this minimum, writers are free to express whatever beliefs they may have as their own understanding, provided that the aim in so doing is to further the object of The Open Bible Trust. A copy of the doctrinal basis is available on **www.obt.org.uk** or from:

THE OPEN BIBLE TRUST
Fordland Mount, Upper Basildon,
Reading, RG8 8LU, UK

www.ingramcontent.com/pod-product-compliance
Lightning Source LLC
Chambersburg PA
CBHW060658030426
42337CB00017B/2678